AF426407

First Edition: September 2024
ISBN: 9798218319700

A Mighty Mac Production LLC
Long Beach, Ca

Learn more about Little Shirley at www.acollegereunion.com

Little Shirley Goes to School

Created by Carla M. McCullough. Ed.D
Illustrated by Robert A.C. Clemons

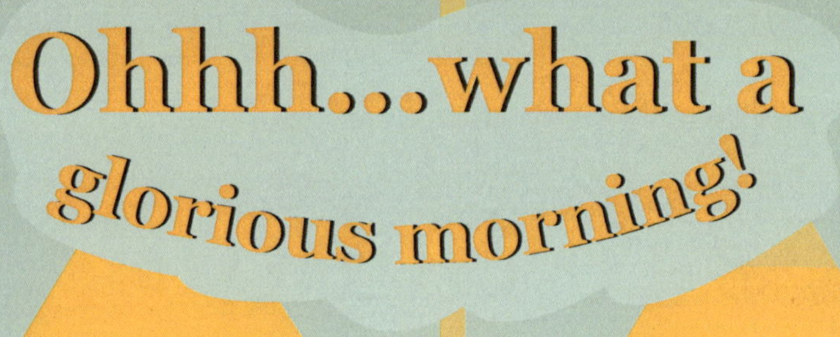

Birds chirped loudly.

The sun shone brightly.
Her whole world seemed happy as can be.

Today would be the
BEST DAY EVER
for Little Shirley.

For today was Monday,

**the 16th day of the
9th month of the year.**

And for the second week in a row
Shirley would be going to **school**.

*Man, how **cool**,*

SEPTEMBER 1963
S M T W T F S
1 2 3 4 5 6 7
8 9 10 11 12 13 14
16 17 18 19 20 21
23 24 25 26 27 28
OCTOBER 1963

is exactly what Little Shirley **thought** as she tied her saddle shoelaces into a **knot**.

She'd just got two new dresses
for school and church.

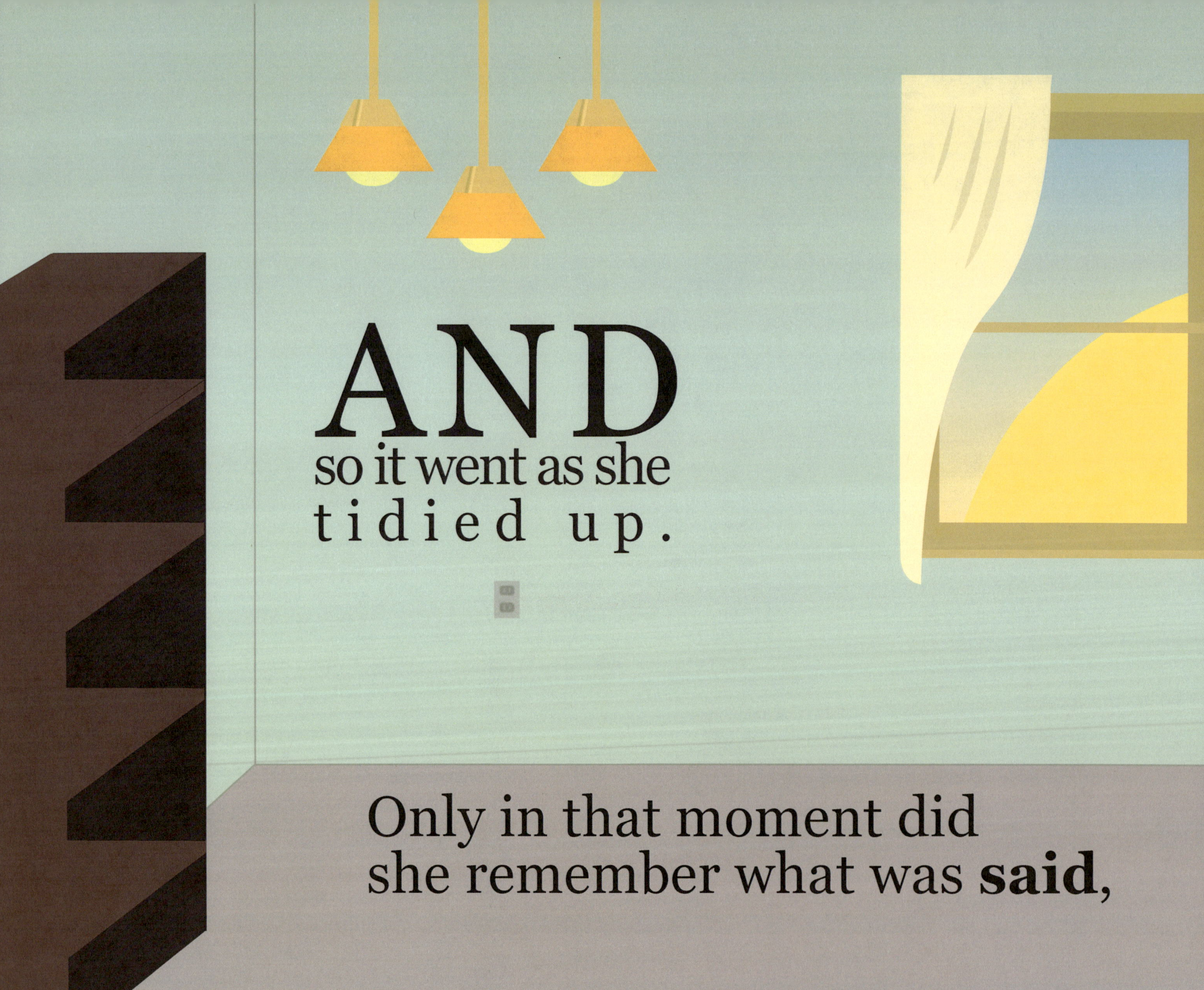

AND
so it went as she
tidied up.
Only in that moment did
she remember what was said,

just last night
on her way
to **bed**.

She thought she heard her mother **say**
That there would be no school **today**.

Nope!

Na uh!

No way!

Not now!

She must have dreamed
that **somehow**.

But when she opened her door,
she heard weeping and wailing, which was
strange.

And it wasn't her baby brother,
who notoriously made a fuss when needing to
be **changed.**

Notorious* was a word that
her teacher helped her spell.

She might have just started school last week,
but she was already starting to excel.

*Notorious: famous or well known, typically for some bad quality or deed.

Maybe cause mama read to her
when papa wasn't **looking**,

from grown up books
and the discarded newspaper
while they were in the kitchen **cooking**.

Cook, Clean, CLEAN, Cook,

Change diapers, hide **books**.

That was her life at home.
Papa said school wasn't a place for little girls.

Good thing

mama disagreed.

For she could never cook, clean,
and change diapers all **day**.

Wait, was that mama weeping and wailing? No **way**.

Maybe she was still asleep...

..and this was all a part of the **dream.**
Just as she turned to go back to her room and start **again,**
Mama called her name much to her **chagrin.**[**]

**chargin: is a feeling of sadness or disappointment.

Shirley

C-H-A-J-R-E-N

Chagrin, did she use it right?
Is it spelled **correctly?**

"Shirley, come over
here and sit
down **directly."**

Mama burst Little Shirley's thought bubble while wiping away tears.

POP

"You okay mama?"
This was strange and she didn't want to **sit**.
She didn't want to see mama cry.
She didn't like it one **bit**.

As she turned her attention from mama to the table she suddenly understood.

"A Flower for the Graves"

Four Black girls were killed.

Stunned, she didn't know how to feel.

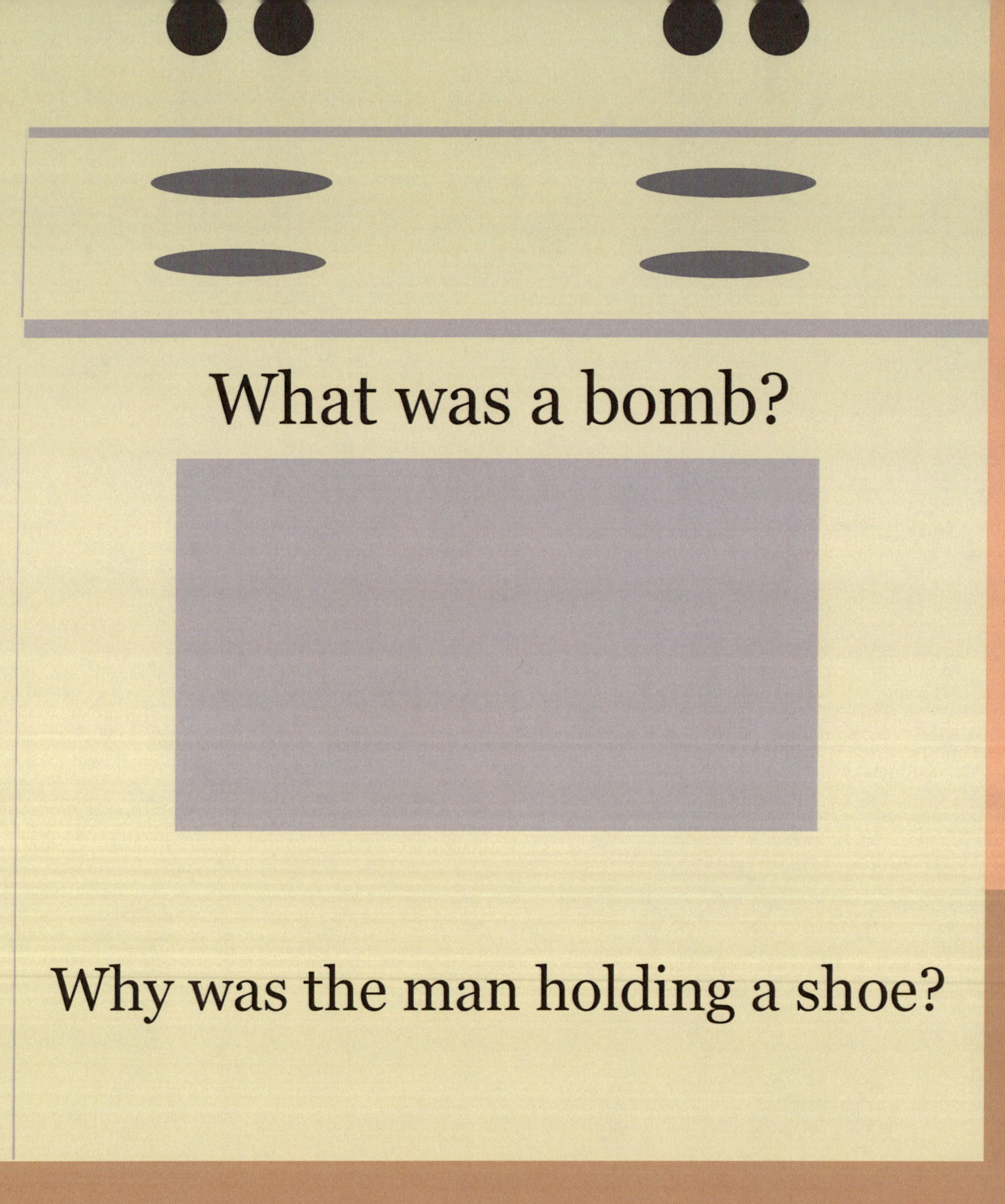

What was a bomb?

Why was the man holding a shoe?

THE ATLANTA DAILY NEWS
FOUR BLACK GIRLS

"**Baby,**
you can't go to school today.

**Actually not
at all this week.**"

This must be a dream or the worst nightmare ever.

Her mother, tears dried now, cut
her down with a **look**.
Little Shirley immediately softened her
tone; she was sufficiently **shook**.

How come, mama?

Because it's my job to keep you **safe**. So we'll just have school at home again, **okay**?

was what Little Shirley thought.

What she said instead was,

So back to her
room
she went.

"Yes, ma'am. Let me go change."

The yellow dress

neatly folded with her nice things.

Everyday house clothes pulled out **again**.

Waaa....

WaaaWaa...

Waaa....

Just outside her door, she heard the familiar SOUND of a baby boy weeping.

Deja vu **began**.

**Time for Little Shirley
to go to school.**

Help mama change diapers,
clean, and cook.

And every
two hours
pull out a book.

She'd listen to mama read
during the first block.
Then read to mama at the second.

By the third chunk of time, they'd be on to the news. Mama quietly read her the front page **tale**.

By now she had no more energy to **wail**.

Mama was just simply **glad**
that the bit of education she **had**
would keep Little Shirley safe for one more day.

That night as Little Shirley lay in **bed**.
All sorts of thoughts ran through her **head**.

But what she wondered most of **all**
was if she'd be able to go back to real school
next **fall**.

Little Shirley's next day of school.
September 26, 1963

www.ingramcontent.com/pod-product-compliance
Lightning Source LLC
Chambersburg PA
CBRC100746110726
48006CB00011B/1443